What Maggie May Did Today

A poem captioned book full of timeless treasures that are fun for everyone.

Inspired from Maggie's daily adventures while needing few expenditures.
Full of discoveries for all dog lovers and lovers of nature.
From Lombard to our great backyard.
Keeping it local is the main point of focal.

Let's follow the sun and have some fun until the day is done.

I know where we are going
and it's where
the river's flowing.

Oh sun shine on me
for it's great to be Maggie.

Around the bend come me and my best friend.

I think I hear a train a coming. I feel a vibration that's humming.

What is the light at the end of the tunnel that looks like a giant funnel?

Here I come, the
u l t i m a t e
river bum.

This dog's day is every day.

I dug us a hole, so our time won't be dull.

I see you Mr. Heron so blue.

A little dirt never hurt.

I want to be a ship.
They're always in the water
ready to dip.

It's hard to nip at an
incoming ship.

O H J O Y!
Land a hoy.

I think it would be
c l e v e r
to live like this
f o r e v e r.

I dropped my ball.
Hopefully my
thrower won't stall.

This dog's no
f o o l.
She knows how to stay
c o o l.

Dad, please come quick.
I need you
to throw my stick.

Never mind the stick.
The end of the log
is what I pick.

Is this mutt an artist,
or what?

This dog don't need a pool.
Just play in the shade and
Be Cool.

Don’t worry about me.
I’m cool to the ‘T’.

If my Dad can go there,
then I too, must dare.

As far as I can see, out there is where I
l o v e to be f r e e.

It's nice to find some solitude
in a world filled with attitude.
So good to get away
at least once a day.

This photo sings,
"I wish I had wings."

Look Dad, I'm a tugboat in a white coat.

Dog with white coat or billy goat?

I love to walk at the pace of a snail,
down the ol' dirt trail.

I don't see any trains, just a
lot of writing from crazy brains.

Under the bridge there are snacks you won't find in the fridge. Everywhere we take walks, opportunity knocks.

There's nothing
a b o v e
this good dog's
l o v e.

There's lots to smile about when you're looking down the end of this snout.

Doesn’t it look pretty to have the background of the city.

An elephant with
a sword
is not to be
ignored.

If I see a shark,
I'll bark.

I'll put my steak
on the snake
for the title take.

We could live here next year. Can we Dad?
Can we live here?

Out here, there's not one kitty,
but in the distance I can see my city.

Life is good
in my hood.

I'm queen of the
concrete jungle.
Although I am small,
up here I feel tall.

Rain or shine.
I'll walk the line.

G e e! There's so much to see.

The bridge lover
finds another cover.

I can smell the
m e m o r i e s
in the trees.

It seems there's never a warner
for what lies around the corner.

Say ‘cheese’.
Next train to
St. John’s
P L E A S E.

Chew, chew,
or is it choo, choo?

Walk no more my legs of four.

If you are ever to discuss,
make sure to give peace to us.

Happy as can be.
This is the
l i f e
for me.

Here comes the top dog,
like a tugboat through the fog.

I skate too.
I thought you knew.

Now I see. The light at the end of the tunnel is M E.

We keep it true,
the one man
and one dog crew.

Maggie here.

Get out and
p l a y.
Don't wait
another day.

About Scott and Maggie

Maggie's dad is Scott Raymond Majors, known as Scizo to his friends. The name Scizo is Scott's old Burnside Bridge nickname. If asked, he says he is everyone and no one. Scizo has always been on his own path and followed his heart, regardless of what trials came his way, and there have been many. At an early age Scizo felt compelled to follow his freedom path doing what he wanted to do. What he wanted to do was skateboard, hang out with friends, and have fun. He wanted to live passionately, to be alive in ways that most people couldn't conceive.

Scizo didn't find school inspiring. It didn't speak his language or tap into his creativity so he left school early in his senior year to live the life of a skateboarder. When he dropped out he also dropped off of mainstream society's radar, not talking with family for months at a time, a move that motivated his mother to buy him his first cellphone. Between that and the adoption of his sweet little Pit-mix Maggie May, Scizo began to move back from the extremes to the closer-in fringes of society. Ask him and he will tell you that Maggie May saved him.

Scizo's chosen lifestyle gave him many unique outlooks on life and at the same time helped him grow into a better person, someone who tries to keep his head straight on his shoulders, what Scizo calls a more solid human. His experiences have allowed him to see himself in the other guy and are a strong influence on his poetry, video, photography and art.

As one might expect, Scizo and Maggie May won't often be seen on society's sidewalks. Most every day they will be off the beaten track, taking the trail less traveled, discovering and exploring all Portland's big back yard has to offer.

Ten percent of the profits from sales of "What Maggie May Did Today" goes to Pitbull awareness and rescue efforts. Thank you for supporting Scott's Maggie May and all the other beautiful Pitbulls so deserving of loving homes and an accepting society.

You can contact Scott at:

ScizoArt.com
scott@scizoart.com